ALISTAIR ROWAN

The Creation of Shambellie

THE STORY OF A VICTORIAN BUILDING CONTRACT

"Enlightened liberality in good time is real economy in the end"

James Duncan to William Stewart, 14 January 1860

1982

Acknowledgments

MY principal debt in the preparation of this short booklet is to Charles Stewart of Shambellie for generously permitting me to borrow the bundles of papers relating to the building of the house, for answering most meticulously my many questions about his estate and for correcting a number of errors. I have also received much help from Miss Naomi Tarrant of the Royal Scottish Museum, from Miss Catherine Cruft of the Royal Commission of Ancient and Historical Monuments of Scotland and from Mr John Pinkerton who guided me on legal matters. I am especially grateful to my wife who suggested many improvements in the text and to my secretary, Mrs Blathnait Crowley who has typed the text quickly and with her usual intuitive sense of what it was I meant to say. The photographs which illustrate the booklet have been taken by Mr Ken Smith, The Royal Scottish Museum. David Bryce's architectural drawings have been presented by Mr Stewart to the Royal Scottish Museum, while the photographs of Victorian interiors and of members of the Stewart family are from Mr Stewart's collection. The photograph and bust of David Bryce come from the collection of the Scottish National Portrait Gallery and the picture of the servants at Capenoch is reproduced by kind permission of Mr Robert Gladstone. To Mr Stewart I owe an additional debt of gratitude for entering so willingly, and to such evident good purpose, into the idea that the booklet would not be complete without some illustrations by himself. It was his work as an illustrator that prompted the formation of the costume collection out of which the opening of Shambellie to the public and thus the very existence of this booklet grew.

Alistair Rowan

Contents

Preface	6
Foreword	6
Dramatis Personae	9
Shambellie and the Stewarts	11
The House	15
Architect and Client	20
The Drawings for Shambellie	28
The Contractors	35
The House goes up	39
Disagreements	44
Settling the Accounts	51
Epilogue	57

Preface

THIS booklet, prepared as a companion to Mr Charles Stewart's *Holy Greed*, is published by the Royal Scottish Museum to mark the opening of Shambellie House as a museum of costume and to commemorate Mr Stewart's notable gift of his collection and house to the Nation. We are grateful to Professor Alistair Rowan of University College, Dublin, for the time he has given to sorting through the documents that relate to the house and for writing this account of the building.

Norman Tebble
Director

Foreword

THE mansion house and estate of Shambellie, which focuses on the village of New Abbey some seven miles south of Dumfries, offers visitors a perfect microcosm of the world of a minor landed gentleman in mid-Victorian Scotland. The house, a Scottish Baronial mansion on a modest scale, is typical of hundreds of similar buildings newly erected, or conjured out of older homes, by go-ahead proprietors throughout the whole of Scotland. Costing just under £3000 in 1862 it was not, by the standards of the time, an expensive house, though its owner, William Stewart, felt it had cost him too much and as a result became involved in acrimonious disputes which wasted much of his time. In this respect the house is perhaps more typical of the world of nineteenth-century builders than it should be, but whether new mansions normally caused trouble or not, Shambellie is unique in the quantity of documents that have survived to chart the course of its creation. The picture that emerges from them is certainly vivid and it may also teach the moral expressed in Victorian language on the title page of this booklet that a generous attitude to expense may, in the long run, be a saving.

Shambellie as it stands today has survived intact, without significant alteration, since 1855. In 1977, through the generosity of Mr Charles Stewart, great-grandson of the original builder, the house was given to the Nation to house Mr Stewart's costume collection which he presented to the Royal Scottish Museum, Edinburgh. The interest of the building is thus twofold: it is maintained as an attractive and highly representative example of a class of Victorian domestic architecture that is now fast disappearing, and it will display in its public rooms a selection of Mr Stewart's important and valuable collection of clothes which is in itself the work of a lifetime. Mr Stewart has written a separate guide book to describe the formation of the costume collection, and it is this collection, formed by a member of the family for whom the house was built, that will be the reason for most visitors going to Shambellie. Yet the claim of the house to an interest in its own right is far from negligible. This booklet by Professor Alistair Rowan is intended to give some account of the building itself and of the personalities involved in its construction. It describes how Shambellie was used, how it came into being, and how the owner, the architect and the builders related one to another. They lived in an energetic, purposeful age and, even if they did not see eye to eye, it is an invigorating experience to follow the consequences and resolution of their actions and to enter imaginatively into the busy world they knew.

R. Oddy
Keeper
Department of Art & Archaeology

Dramatis Personae

William Stewart of Shambellie, *a country gentleman*
Katherine Hardie, *his wife*
James Duncan, *his family lawyer in Edinburgh*
Robert K. Walker, *his lawyer in Dumfries*

David Bryce, *a successful architect in Edinburgh*
James Campbell Walker, *chief clerk to Mr Bryce*
John Paris, *a clerk in Mr Bryce's office*

William Lawrence, *an ordained surveyor, brother-in-law to Mr Bryce*
Francis Kedslie, *a clerk of works sent by Mr Bryce to Shambellie*
James Kay, *another clerk of works sent by Mr Bryce to Shambellie*

Joseph Robson, *a small building contractor from Carsethorn, Kirkcudbrightshire*
Thomas Walker ⎫
William Walker ⎬ *masons from Dalbeattie, working for Mr Robson*
James Carew ⎭
John Mein, *a carpenter in Dumfries*
John Hill, *a carpentry contractor from Juniper Green, Edinburgh*
William Anderson, *a slating contractor in Edinburgh*
James Anderson, *a plasterer in Edinburgh*
John McIlraith, *a plumber in Ayr*
J. B. McMorrice, *a painter*
Thomas Costins, *another painter*
Robert Bell, *a bell-hanger in Dumfries*
James Carruthers, *a monumental mason in Carlisle*
James Lewis, *a mason employed to replace Mr Robson*
James Montgomery, *a builder in Dumfries, employed to replace Mr Robson*

Andrew Scott, C. E., *an architect in Dumfries*
William Reid Corson, *an architect in Manchester*
John Barbour, *another architect in Dumfries*

M. J. Stuart, *Mr Robson's lawyer in Edinburgh*

Choosing the site, July 1854.

Shambellie and the Stewarts

WILLIAM Stewart of Shambellie who built Shambellie House between 1856 and about 1860 was head of a family of minor Scottish landowners whose ancestors had been associated with Galloway from early in the fifteenth century. The Shambellie branch of the Stewarts traced its descent through Sir William Stewart of Garlies, born in 1410, to Walter, High Steward of Scotland in the twelfth century, and beyond him to the Stewart forbears in Brittany who had acted as governors of the royal household for the Dukes of Normandy at Dol. There was therefore nothing *nouveau* about Mr Stewart. The house that he planned to build was not a prestigious symbol of commercial or industrial self-advancement as were so many new mansions in the early Victorian age. If anything it was part of an attempt to rationalise his estate, to cater for the needs of his family with an up-to-date plan and possibly—almost incidentally—to reflect the credit of a certain modernity upon his way of life.

The property that made up the Shambellie estate had belonged to Sweetheart Abbey. At the Reformation, when the threat of confiscation hung over most church property, the last two abbots, an uncle and nephew called Brown, disposed of the lands which later became Shambellie to relations to prevent them from falling into the hands of the crown. In 1625 the Stewarts

1. William Stewart aged about 30.

acquired the estate from the Browns and in the course of time the abbot's house in New Abbey village became their family home. From this time on the Stewarts of Shambellie had occupied a modest station amongst the landed interests of South West Scotland. One forbear of Mr Stewart's, William Stewart, had risen to the position of Lord Mayor of London in 1721 while his nephew, another William and ultimately the heir to Shambellie, had followed the tradition implicit in the family's name, acting as Secretary and Chamberlain to the powerful Dukes of Queensberry whose territorial interests radiated throughout the South West.

It was this William, Secretary to the Queensberry Dukes, who was the ancestor of the Victorian family at Shambellie. The line of descent passed through his second son Charles who had married a Miss Anne Hay by whom he had two sons, William and James, and it is Charles and his son William who dominate the eighteenth-century history of the estate. The father, a worthy man of enterprise and initiative, built up his property to an estate of some 2400 acres; began the plantations for which Shambellie was to become famous; and

2. Katherine Hardie about the time of her marriage to William Stewart in 1845: miniature by John Faed.

developed his commercial interests. With two Dumfries merchants he formed a company that traded in Scandinavia, the Low Countries and in America. He built a town house in Dumfries and a snuff mill at Glenharvie, on the Shambellie estate, where tobacco imported from Virginia was ground to a powder and re-exported as snuff. The son William, born in 1750 and his father's heir in initiative and drive, was destined to become one of those patriarchal figures in which the Scottish eighteenth century abounds. In 1773 when he was 23, he took over control of the estate, remaining to direct its development for 71 years, which straddled four reigns and carried a note of Georgian vigour and full-blooded living well into the Victorian age. By his first wife he had fifteen children, and there were also bastards by several local girls. In 1792 to secure the succession of the estate he executed an entail and then, on the death of his only surviving son, Charles, in 1807 married a second wife, Bethia Donaldson, when he was already almost 60 years old. By Bethia he had four sons and three daughters the youngest of whom was born when his father was 70. He survived his second wife to marry a third, Jessie Howat, by whom he had no children though he lived to the age of 94 and did not die until 1844.

William Stewart of Shambellie, the builder of the Victorian house, was the second and eldest surviving son of his father's second marriage. He was born in 1815 and came into the estate when he was 29 years old. It is never easy to succeed a vigorous and enterprising parent while to be the child of an elderly man carries its own burden. With a gap of 65 years between his father and himself, the young William can have had little opportunity to manage his own affairs before he became laird. As a man of 24 he attended the flamboyant Romantic fiasco of the Eglinton tournament dressed in medieval costume and accompanied by a family retainer 'Old Paton' whose one recorded comment, that he was 'the bonniest wee laird o' them a', though touching and no doubt affectionate in intention, hardly suggests that in 1839 he exercised much authority in his father's household. In 1845, within a year of taking over, William Stewart was married. His bride, Katherine, was the daughter of a Mr John Hardie of Leith, and by her he had at least seven children, six of whom survived into adult life. For several years, while the Shambellie family grew, Katherine and William lived together in the Early Georgian surrounding of the Stewarts' old home. Mr Stewart learnt the business of his estate and prudently put aside a portion of his total income, valued at some £1,500 a year, against the cost of a more modern house. Then in 1854, ten years after he had come into his own, the great adventure began: an architect was appointed, plans were drawn up and the building of Shambellie was set in hand. This was the moment for the realisation of a long cherished ideal, yet for William Stewart there was to be little or no satisfaction in the creation of his new home. Indeed among Victorian country houses in Scotland, Shambellie is uniquely unfortunate in its building history. Almost everything that could go wrong with its construction did so. Mr Stewart fell out with his architect, the tradesmen he had employed, his friends and almost everybody connected with the house. In the end he was brought to court by his builder. Yet if Shambellie is a lesson on the vanity of human wishes, in another sense it is a monument to William Stewart's economy and care. The very fact that so much went wrong, despite his best endeavour, has given the story of his house an interest far beyond the intrinsic value of its design. Had the contract run smoothly we might now know very little about the design and building of Shambellie: because it did not, there accumulated a mass of detailed and specific documents through which we may begin to understand the world of Victorian builders in Scotland.

3. Shambellie from the North West.

The House

IN many ways Shambellie House is typical of what moderately well-to-do people regarded as an ideal home in early Victorian Scotland. A completely new house on a new site, its style and situation reflect the conscious choice of William Stewart and Katherine, his wife, and of their architect, the principal country-house designer in Scotland at that time, David Bryce. Mr Stewart and Bryce corresponded extensively both about the design of the house and on the progress of the building once the design had been fixed. Their letters are full of opinions as to what was or was not desirable in a gentleman's residence at that time and, from them, a very detailed picture emerges as to how Shambellie was intended to be used.

The mansion was to be built on a raised bank in Shambellie woods to take advantage of a spectacular view across the estate to Criffel, a round-topped hill which rises to the south west. William Stewart at first had had two sites in

4. Shambellie from the South West.

mind. He inspected both of them with his architect in July 1854 when Bryce had come across for an afternoon while on business in the area at Capenoch and Closeburn Tower. It was Bryce who decided that Shambellie should be built where it stands today. 'I have no hesitation whatever about the site of the house' he wrote in October the same year. The one in the woods, was 'the most picturesque in the country' and could 'be made perfectly beautiful'. The other was too low, too near a road and—the 'fatal objection' in Bryce's view—too close to the boundary line of the estate to be able to enjoy the sort of privacy that was proper for a private gentleman.

The mixture of picturesque and practical considerations which dictated the choice of the site is reflected in the appearance and the layout of the house itself. Shambellie is conceived romantically as an old Scottish manor house. Its massing is irregular and its details with stone-mullioned bay-windows, crow-stepped gables and conical roof turrets, are those of sixteenth and seventeenth-century Scottish vernacular building. This particular style was felt to be appropriate for mountainous and dramatic scenery and was one which Bryce had made peculiarly his own. No doubt, when William Stewart

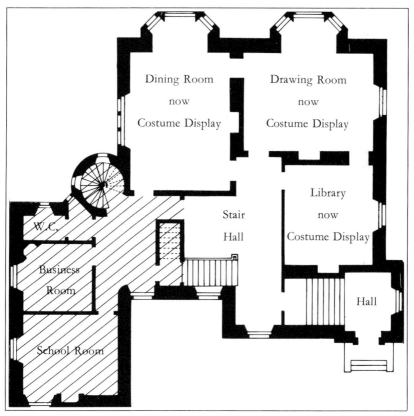

5. Plan of the main floor of the house.

first met the architect he would have asked him to produce a design in his Scottish Baronial manner. Bryce also had a reputation for designing convenient and well thought out houses which would have recommended him further to his client. Shambellie, even though the original design had to be cut down in execution, is still a characteristic and neat example of his planning.

Perhaps the most striking feature of the present building, apart from its architectural style, is the way in which the house is tucked into a fall in the ground so that it appears to be one storey higher from the gardens to the south and west. This simple expedient, which is a common Bryce device, achieves several ends in one: from the exterior it gives the building much more consequence than a conventional basement or 'sunk storey' would do; it provides the servants, accommodated in the ground floor, with far better rooms than they were usually given in Victorian houses; and it gives to the proprietor, his family and friends, a main floor lifted high above the garden level so that it is at once private and yet enjoys, through generous bay windows, unimpeded views of the surrounding countryside.

A primary aim in the planning of a Victorian mansion, even on the modest scale of Shambellie, was to identify the needs of the three broad classes of inhabitants in a house—family, servants and visitors—and to devise as far as possible separate circulation routes within the house for each class. Visitors to Shambellie today are confined to almost precisely the same rooms as the guests of William and Katherine Stewart would have been shown when the house was newly finished in the early 1860s. The entrance hall is set at the north west corner of the building, half a floor below the level of the main rooms and shut off from them by a stout draught-excluding door. It is placed consciously at the extreme end of the entrance front while at the other, shielded by the projection of a short wing, is the entrance for servants and tradesmen which is at a lower level and is approached by a short back drive. The split level of the entrance hall is really an idea left over from Bryce's first proposal for the house when, before economies had reduced the design, he had intended to provide a half flight of stair from the basement to the front hall to permit a servant to answer the main door bell without having to cross the stair hall or any of the 'public' areas of the house, a segregation which he considered desirable in any well regulated household. Within the main building the library and drawing room and dining room were arranged in an L-shaped suite, each with separate access to the stair hall, while the main stair itself went no further than the first floor.

While the areas served by the main hall and stair marked the limit of a visitor's knowledge of Shambellie, the Stewarts and their servants could make use of a separate spiral staircase, set in a round tower in the angle between the main house and the projecting wing on the North East. This stair gave access through the full height of the building from the staff in the basement to the nursery wing and the maids' bedrooms in the attic.

The north east wing, projecting from a corner of the main block, is another idea that is typical of Bryce. This was to be the family wing, the private domain of the proprietor and his wife who could, if they chose, get away from their guests should the need arise. And of course it did. Guests are not always welcome and, if they are, can stay too long. Victorian families such as Mr Stewart's while often very large were limited in their acquaintance to persons of their own position which, in provincial society, as often as not left a quantity of younger sons or daughters doomed to live singly and, in their later years, in the homes of their brother's children. The perpetual semi-resident uncle or aunt was one of the hazards of Victorian life in the country and Bryce, like other architects of his period, thought it as well to plan for this contingency. Thus at Shambellie the Stewarts had private rooms with direct and separate access both to their staff and to their dining room without the necessity of going into the public areas of the house. As was the case with the entrance hall, the family wing had to be modified considerably in the house as built. In his first proposals Bryce had designed a third 'family stair', an idea that seems to have much appealed to Mr Stewart who disliked bumping into nannies and small children in his house, and a complete suite of bedroom, dressing room, bathroom and boudoir all on the main floor. But here the architect's notion of what was appropriate ran ahead of that of his clients, particularly when expense became a problem. In the house as built the family wing was reduced, at main floor level, to no more than an embryo of Bryce's original conception. In effect it became the nursery wing and exists today as a passage, the old school room, a business room and a lavatory. Yet its presence at all demonstrates clearly the principle of division by use of the different parts of a Victorian house.

The conversion of the main rooms of Shambellie to serve as a museum has robbed them of their principal feature, the splendid views which they once commanded across the grounds and lower borders of the policies, for the display and protection of the costumes have made it necessary to block out all daylight. A visitor can still appreciate the extent of window openings in each room and note the architect's care in providing a sunny dining room for breakfast, with its large east facing mullioned-window, and the south and west windows in the drawing room and library which catch all the evening light. A house by Bryce is usually pleasant to live in and most of the architect's clients were well satisfied with his work. William Stewart of Shambellie was unfortunately an exception. Even before the house was begun he had become alarmed about its cost; as a result the interior is far less elaborate than Bryce would have wished: modest plaster cornices replace the ornate bracketed designs intended for the main rooms; embellishments in the masonry are omitted; deal is substituted for oak; the chimney-pieces are not by Bryce but by a jobbing mason from Carlisle; and finally, to achieve a saving of a few feet in the banisters, the main stair has been turned to run in the opposite direction to that which Bryce intended, a last minute alteration that made the first flight

6. David Bryce from a photograph taken about 1860.

pass clumsily across one of the windows of the entrance front. Bryce would normally have avoided such an awkward compromise but by the time the stair was altered he had lost interest in the job; the whole commission was in a mess, and Stewart was thoroughly dissatisfied with his architect, his builder and almost everyone connected with the house.

Architect and Client

MR Stewart's new mansion house at Shambellie, with David Bryce as its architect, was first discussed as a possibility towards the end of July 1854. It was then that Bryce came down to visit his client for the first time, and the two men walked about the estate and inspected, as we have seen, two alternative sites. We do not know in detail what they said to each other but from the correspondence that has survived about the design and building of the house we can reconstruct a little of what was agreed. As the business was soon to be enmeshed in misunderstanding and ultimately in complete disagreement, it is as well at the outset to have a clear idea of what each expected of the other, but

7. A daguerrotype of William Stewart about 1855.

before considering William Stewart's instructions we should perhaps look at the two men who were tramping together in the woodlands near New Abbey. With hindsight it is quite clear that Bryce and Stewart were fundamentally unsuited to each other.

David Bryce in 1854 was 51 years old. Already at the height of his profession, he was far too big an architect to take the sort of trouble with a smallish design which his client expected that he should and Stewart was much too much of a fuss-pot not to get under his skin. As Bryce had risen in the world—his family connections were with building tradesmen in late Georgian Edinburgh—his sense of style and of his own position had developed also. In his youth his letters had been sealed with a simple monogram DB, but the correspondence that issued from his office at 131 George Street, Edinburgh, to William Stewart and to numerous and more substantial patrons in the 1850s, bore a crest of a naked arm brandishing a sword encircled by a motto, DO WELL DOUBT NOT. When a man bestows a crest upon himself it presumably reflects his nature closely, and in Bryce's case the self-assertive character of the emblem and motto merge perfectly with the man. With his clients he was direct, not to say blunt. The scale of his works had made him decisive by habit and it was not usual for him either to mince or to waste his words.

Mr Stewart was different. In 1854 he was 39, twelve years younger than his architect; both his experience and the sphere of his operations were more limited. He had set his heart on having a new house and he had approached Bryce in the expectation that he would give him the best design. No doubt he enjoyed notions of patronage and of employing a fashionable architect. Shambellie was undoubtedly the most ambitious venture in which he had so far been involved, but it was also one which he felt he could only barely afford. In his very first communication with Bryce in May that year he had been careful to ask what his fees would be for visiting the site and preparing designs for a house. Even at the outset the cost of Shambellie was a problem yet, had William Stewart only asked a little further he might have found out that the architect on whom his choice had fallen was not noted for being careful with his clients' cash.

At the meeting on the site Stewart requested Bryce to prepare designs for a Scottish Baronial country house and indicated, in a general sort of way, what accommodation he would require. Bryce asked about the extent of the domestic offices and suggested that, to add to the picturesque effect and to give more consequence to the design, a stable block should be incorporated into the main group and not be built separately on its own. He thought a house such as he had in mind could be built for £3,000. That was more than William Stewart intended to spend and he asked Bryce to limit his proposals to a house of £2,000. What he meant by the term 'house' was not spelt out however, and at the end of the meeting both men parted with a rather different notion of what had been agreed between them.

Any client is naturally anxious, having instructed an architect, to see what he will propose. After opening negotiations in May it must have been a little disappointing for Mr Stewart to find the autumn almost over without any news from Bryce. Accordingly he wrote, on 17 October 1854, to ask what had become of the plans for his new house. Bryce replied, perhaps a little grandly that his being 'obliged to go to the Continent' had held up the designs but promised to send them in a week or ten days. On 1 November sketch plans were sent from the office in Edinburgh together with a letter explaining the working of the rooms and giving some basic measurements. Bryce was keen to know whether the arrangement met with the Stewarts' views adding, almost as an afterthought, 'everything is made as small as it can with propriety be made and I do not think there should be less accommodation'. Following the plans an attractive perspective sketch of the house from the South East (8) was sent ten days later; and then a week after that a second view, from the North West, together with a brief letter stating that the probable estimate of the cost of the house, prepared by an Edinburgh surveyor, was for £3,000 with a further £700 for the stable offices.

The tone of Bryce's letters at this time suggests that he realised the design was beyond his client's means. Although the price allowed for the whole building to be executed 'with foreign timber in the very best way and for finishing the rooms handsomely' he was at pains to point out, when sending a subsequent 'detailed probable estimate', that the cost could be brought down by using Shambellie timber instead of imported woods.

Early in December Stewart wrote back to ask for a breakdown of the costs between the materials and the labour. Evidently he liked the design and now, like many of Bryce's clients, found himself in the agonising position either of having to settle for a reduced house, or else of having to find more cash. His first reaction was to wonder if he could save on materials: the stone and the timber, and to attempt to persuade himself that building in the country would cost less than in the capital. Bryce suggested that if the price of the home timber could be brought to a shilling a cubic foot 'the house as it stood upon the plans would cost between £2,700 and £2,800'. He could also cut out some embellishments and curtail the kitchen and stable offices a little. To come to a final decision he would recommend that the working plans should be prepared and proper estimates taken. On 19 December Stewart replied agreeing to these proposals: 'If you think by these alterations you can curtail the estimates within my limits, I have no objection to your preparing working plans and obtaining estimates'. If this could not be done 'there would be no use in incurring such an expense and trouble'. The sum of £2,500 must cover 'the cost of the house ready for papering and painting' with 'all incidental expenses'. This was £500 more than he had intended but then 'the offices' had not been included.

It was not perhaps Bryce's intention that Shambellie should have worked out at much more than his client had laid down, yet the correspondence which now began to flow between Kirkcudbrightshire and Edinburgh was of a type that often occurred in the George Street office. Experience had taught the architect that proprietors in Scotland tended to be canny and to underestimate what they could afford to spend on a house. A number had very compliantly agreed to extra expense thereby securing a better design for their families and a better fee for Bryce, so it was perhaps an office ploy—to put it no more strongly—to design generously and readjust the price later. If this was the intention at Shambellie, the stratagem was ill conceived with a client like William Stewart.

Bryce soon found himself caught up in a tedious wrangle about the home grown timber which Stewart wanted to have the contractor cut down for himself while Bryce, who thought this was hopelessly unbusinesslike, 'took it for granted that it would be furnished ready cut' in appropriate sizes for use as joists and rafters. By the end of January 1855 a tetchy note that was to recur in much of the Shambellie correspondence already makes itself felt: 'You take an erroneous view of the expense of sawing timber; the average cost for carpentry purposes in house building does not exceed 2d. per cubic foot when cut by hand, and must be a great deal less when done by machinery, and the difference between your timber and foreign timber would not be above 6d. sawn, so that it would be better to use foreign timber rather than make such a paltry saving.'

Much later in the history of Shambellie, when William Stewart had become quite disillusioned with builders and architects, his views about the building were to be expressed not by himself but by his wife. As it was she who then undertook to write letters on his behalf, we may not be wide of the mark if we allow her a significant role in the opening stages of the story, for Stewart's next letter to Bryce bears all the traces of conjugal debate. So far as the timber is concerned the husband takes a disarmingly lofty stand. He wishes to be advised only on which would be the best timber to choose. He has Scots fir, larch and 'plenty of oak for lintels'; the saving on the wood is not so vital. But what of the plans? Evidently the Stewarts have been thinking very carefully about the reality of their own style of living and have compared it with what is suggested in the Bryce design. Wasn't there much more here than they really required? More could be pared away. The kitchens could be brought up to the main floor level instead of being in a basement. There were too many water closets. The maids could sleep in the attics. And, on reflection had it been wise to go as far as £2,500? That was extravagance. Mr Stewart would now revert to his opinion that the house 'including of course the kitchen offices' should be built for £2,000.

For Bryce the time had evidently come to clear the air. 'I fear that we misunderstand each other', he wrote by return of post. 'When I was at Shambellie, I understood that the price that you were willing to expend on the house was £2,400. At this time the stables were not understood to be in connection with the house. I afterwards recommended that the stables should be made in connection with the house as they would add much to the apparent extent. In your letter of 19th October last you again mention that you would not like the expense to exceed £2,500, including the offices, which I concluded were the kitchen offices, as they had been kept separate in the estimate sent to you. However in your letter of yesterday you speak of £2,000 being the expense of the house, which at once leads me to understand that you intended the £2,500 to cover the expense of the stable offices. Now if this is the case my labour is lost because it is impossible to make a house of the description for £2,000.... My intention, if a curtailment were required to take place, was to have arranged the kitchen offices under the main building, which is marked on the basement plan by the pencil lines, and in this way I think the house could be built for the £2,400 or £2,500—but certainly not with the stable offices included—of course, if a £2,000 house is wished, the plans will be totally different.'

The draft of Stewart's reply, of the 5th February 1855, is written immediately on the back of Bryce's letter, in a rapid hand and with many underlinings: 'I have yours of the 3rd inst. as also the working drawings and am extremely sorry to find that from the simple misunderstanding of *a technicality of expression* so much valuable time and trouble have been wasted. It never occurred to me that the kitchen offices were a separate estimate from the dwelling house for I did not suppose a house could be completed *without kitchen accommodation* and, in speaking of offices, I have always meant the stables, coach-houses etc. detached from the main buidling. In your letter of the 15th Dec., you say the house as it stands upon the plans would cost between £2,700 and £2,800, if the timber for the carpentry purposes was furnished at the price you name of one shilling per cubic foot. Now, I looked upon the plans as comprehending *the whole building* on the plans which embraced the stable offices, and in the P.S. of my letter of the 19th, in answer, I said I wished £2,500 to cover all incidental expenses connected with the erection of the house meaning the whole building on the plan. ... I still hope you will be able to modify the plans so as to meet my views. I should not like much less accommodation on the bedroom plan, but the family bedroom and dressing room on the principal plan may be dispensed with, and I think if the whole of the public rooms were arranged in one line or suite looking East, the space in that storey might be much economised as I don't care about a bedroom on the principal floor'. (Poor Bryce who had made such a study of the arrangement of public and private rooms must have wondered at his client now!) 'What I have *all along wanted* is a house for £2,000, not including stable offices, but every other accommodation pertaining to a dwelling house and when you talked of £3,000 when you were here I said it was too much.

You had better leave the stables entirely out of the estimates, as I have always considered the stable offices a secondary consideration, and thus I shall hear from you definitely what is to be done in the course of a day or two'.

The outcome of this letter was that Bryce had virtually to re-design Shambellie. Stewart's day or two stretched to a month with no word from the architect. Then a rather hurt reminder, sent on the 28th February, provoked the response that sketches of the house on a reduced scale would be sent within the next week. In the letter that accompanied the new plan (sent in fact a fortnight later) Bryce explained that he had reduced everything to as compact a design as possible. The kitchen wing had become a coal cellar and the women servants' rooms were in the attics. He had built a similar house to what he now proposed a few years previously for £1,850 so he expected that the new Shambellie would not exceed Stewart's limits. It was perhaps foolish of Bryce to mention a sum of even £150 less than the Stewarts' limit. Not only were his clients now delighted but Mr Stewart at once began to suggest additions—a larger kitchen, a school room and a private stair (because of the children)—and he thought the dining room and the drawing room seemed 'rather small'. On his return from a trip to various jobs in the North, Bryce wrote to say that he would make these alterations though they would increase the expense and, soon after, he sent down tracings of the old working drawings altered to the new plan for Stewart's approval which was given by return.

A little later, on the 30th March, Bryce again wrote about the additions. These he thought could add between £200 to £250 to the cost of the building bringing it to a total of £2,100 which, he was careful to point out, would not include his fees as architect nor the cost of superintendence by a Clerk of Works. He would not ink in the working drawings, completed in pencil, until he heard from his client.

Almost from the moment he had approached Bryce, William Stewart had been uneasy about the expense, even the extravagance, of building a new house. Like many a small proprietor before, he wanted to put up a good show but to put it up without straining the estate. There could be no hint of over-spending. He wanted a large house for the price of a small house and, worst of all, he expected that his architect should reassure him that it was all possible. Now without any warning, fees which he had always fancied were included in the price were sprung upon him, *plus* a clerk of works. Together they could carry the cost to £2,384 or almost £400 more than he had first intended. Now he began to fuss about more hidden expenses. Why could Bryce not say plainly what the house would cost?

Throughout April and May letters went back and forth between the two men. Stewart was clearly exasperated and, as he had formed the bad habit of dashing off intemperate replies by return, without time for reflection, a good deal of his exasperation communicated itself in George Street. Bryce in response became increasingly impatient with a minor client whose anxiety and indecision were taking up a disproportionate amount of his time. His tone becomes very firm, displaying even a certain professional indignation at suggestions that he had been wasting time: 'My visit to Shambellie was on the 20th of July last and since then I have prepared designs and one set of working drawings complete—designs and a second set of working drawings have been finished in everything but the putting in ink; in fact my own labour has been entirely expended on them, so that when this is considered, I cannot be charged with having lost time'. As for Stewart's suggestion that he should guarantee the cost of the building, that was ridiculous. It would be quite unusual for an architect 'to come under any undertaking of the cost of a building further than a probable estimate' and he recommended that to ascertain the real cost Stewart should proceed to get actual contract prices from 'responsible men'. Then if the price still proved too high the working drawings could be further modified to reduce the expense again. This to Bryce seemed the only possible course of action: certainly he was not prepared to begin a third design for the house. But Stewart was now thoroughly riled. 'The matter now resolves itself with a question of this kind', he wrote on the 4th April, 'that I must either take an inadequate house or dispense with one all together—I fear I must choose the latter alternative in the meantime, unless a more economical mode can be adopted for its erection'. Three weeks later, as Bryce had not replied, a more moderate letter expressed the hope that something might still be saved out of all Bryce's trouble. Could he perhaps have the working plans completed and then Stewart might get the building erected himself at some subsequent date? And could Bryce please let him know what he was owed?

To Bryce, who in the spring of 1855 was continually on the move under the pressure of several large commissions, the suggestion that Shambellie should be built without his superintendence must have been attractive. On the 11th May he wrote to say that his fees for furnishing working plans, specifications and detailed drawings were 3 per cent of the outlay, provided he had 'no further trouble in the matter' and he should prefer such an arrangement. A Clerk of Works salary would be from 30 shillings to 60 shillings per week according to his experience but one at 30 shillings would be quite sufficient for

8. A perspective view of the first design for Shambellie seen from the South East: sent by David Bryce to William Stewart in November 1854

Shambellie. He would not agree to have any continuing connection with the project himself unless a Clerk of Works were employed. Mr Stewart would have to pay for the first set of designs whatever system were adopted for executing the present plans but, as Bryce was leaving the office the next morning for two or three days, he could not make out an account until his return. Bryce was never an architect to press his clients for payment and in this case he perhaps thought it best to let sleeping dogs lie. He sent in no account. As the summer months of 1855 slipped by nothing more was heard in Edinburgh of Mr Stewart's intended mansion.

The Drawings for Shambellie

ONLY a selection of the drawings that Bryce prepared for Shambellie survives. Of the first scheme which proved too costly, the perspective view from the south east alone remains. Bryce, as we have seen, prepared two views, a set of design plans and a complete set of working drawings between November 1854 and January 1855 but, with the exception of the one view, which the Stewarts framed perhaps as a keepsake of their pipedream, everything was returned to the architect and has since been lost. A comparison between this sketch (8) and Shambellie as built demonstrates clearly the grander scale on which the

9. Shambellie from the South East. The arrangement of the dining-room and drawing-room bay windows remains unaltered from the first design.

design was at first conceived, with the main block, family wing and stable offices descending in a regular progression from West to East. The number of bartizans—the conical roofed corner turrets—and the greater enrichment of the diningroom bay window, with the small gabled bow squashed up against it, are typical picturesque elements in a Bryce scheme—elements which not uncommonly had to be pruned or entirely removed when contractors' tenders were received. At Shambellie the design was to be started again virtually from scratch though the elevation of the main block remained much the same with one feature—the pair of bay windows—which is absolutely characteristic of its architect's manner of design.

Bryce liked his plans to be logical and as far as possible even symmetrical, a legacy of his late-Georgian training with William Burn in Edinburgh. Yet if he sought balance in the disposition of his plan he could artfully disguise it by a picturesque arrangement of the elevation. This is very much the case at Shambellie where the balanced pair of drawing-room and dining-room bay

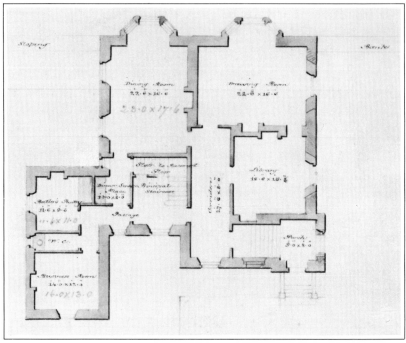

10. Plan of the main floor of Shambellie from the second design client's drawings of March 1855.

windows appear quite differently outside: the one is stopped at first floor level to provide a balcony for the bedroom above it while the other is corbelled out with a projecting gable on the floor above.

More survives of Bryce's second, reduced design. There is a complete set of design drawings for Mr and Mrs Stewart and several working drawings, all of which are typical of Bryce's office practice. The clients' drawings which are on a small scale and give little detail beyond overall measurements are essentially diagrams of the layout of the rooms. The plan of the principal floor, dated 12 March 1855, shows the house which Bryce thought could be built for £1,850. It is instructive to compare this with its equivalent working drawing of October the same year where the additional family stair, added at Mr Stewart's request is incorporated. In the earlier drawing (10) where no secondary stair was envisaged, Bryce has placed the stair in a space of its own separated from the main corridor of the house to minimise the impact of day-

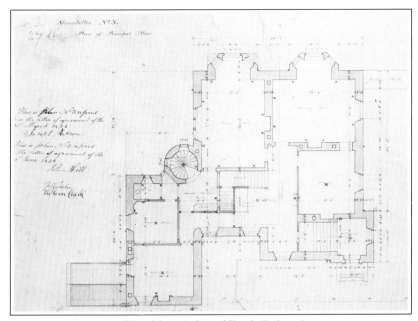

11. Plan of the main floor of Shambellie from the
working drawings of October 1855.
In execution for the sake of minor economies the
direction of the staircase flights was to be reversed— compare 5.

to-day domestic business on the public rooms, but in the later working drawing with the domestic routine removed to the secondary spiral stair, the principal staircase is absorbed into the corridor with a consequent elaboration of picturesque effects within the house. In the revised version of the plan the new spiral stair also becomes the only means of communication between the principal rooms and the servants' quarters on the ground floor. There is no record of the number of women and men who were to be employed as servants by the Stewarts, but the full complement of a Scottish country-house staff about the time that Shambellie was built is vividly recorded in a series of photographs taken at another Bryce house, Capenoch, the seat of Mr T. S. Gladstone not very far away at Penpont in Dumfriesshire. Mr Gladstone's servants and estate workers were to be photographed at least four times in the nineteenth century, and in the earliest group, taken outside the drawing-room bay window about 1860, the typical establishment of a medium-sized country house poses for its picture: the gamekeeper with his gun

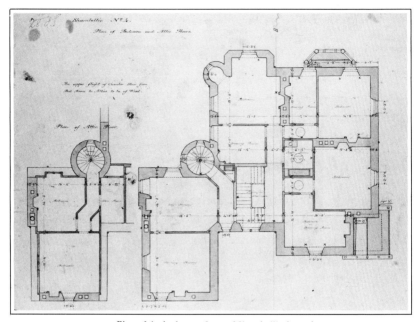

12. Plan of the bedroom floor of Shambellie from the working drawings of October 1855.

13. The Servants at Capenoch, a Scottish-Baronial house built by David Bryce, pictured about 1860.

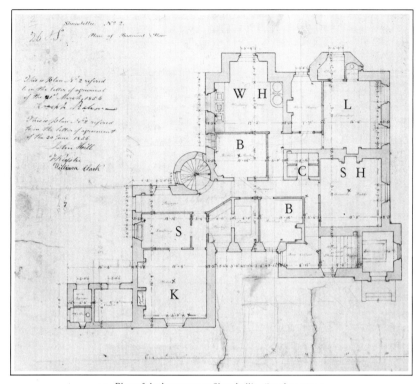

14. Plan of the basement at Shambellie, October 1855:
B. Butler's Pantry and Bedroom; C. Wine and Beer
cellars; K. Kitchen; S. Scullery; S.H. Servants' Hall; L.
Laundry; W. H. Wash House.

and a dead rabbit; the house carpenter with hammer and saw; the gardeners with rakes; the coachman in a top hat; the butler and two raw table-waiters holding dishes, one little more than a boy. The women in the group are the house-keeper, the cook, and the house and laundry maids, together with mature women apparently married to estate workers who probably 'came in' as needed.

Though Shambellie was a smaller house than Capenoch and the Stewarts had probably fewer staff Bryce's arrangements for the servants are carefully planned. In the ground floor of the house there are three departments: the kitchen offices, the wash-house and laundry, and the servants' hall (14). The kitchen (K), a potential source of smells, is located in the wing under the school-room and is isolated from the rest of the house by a lobby off which the scullery opens on one side and the pantry and larder on the other. Immediately opposite this lobby is the stair which connects immediately with both the diningroom and Mr Stewart's business room on the first floor. Thus both the food from the kitchen and tenants or tradesmen who had business with Mr Stewart could be conducted directly, with minimum disruption of the household, to the appropriate rooms. The wash house (WH) and laundry (L) are placed beneath the dining-room and drawing-room as a separate department of the household, and the servants' hall (SH) is underneath the library. For the female servants there is a lavatory opening off the laundry room while that for the men is outside beyond the coal house. The butler, who is ultimately responsible for the behaviour of all domestic staff, is in a key position to supervise the life of the household below-stairs with his pantry and bedroom (BB) on either side of the basement passage in the centre of the house and the beer and wine cellars (CC) nearby. As Victorian practice tended rigidly to segregate domestic staff by sex, it seems likely that at Shambellie the butler was to be the only living-in male servant, for the other staff sleeping quarters are situated all together in the attics.

The workings drawings differ from the design drawings principally in that they provide a quantity of detailed information about how the house is to be built. The masonry is sized to a minimum measurement of half an inch and a conventional colour code—grey for stone, red for brick, yellow for timber and blue for metal or slate—indicates which materials are to be used and where. To complement these plans, and to be read in conjunction with them, the architect prepared a *Specification* or a written description, which laid down standards for the construction and the quality of materials to be used, and it was on the basis of these plans and specification that tradesmen were to be asked to tender for the various contracts which building the house would involve. Even if Shambellie had long ago been demolished—like many other minor houses by Bryce—these plans would be proof that it had once existed. The working drawings are endorsed with the signatures of the men who built the house: Joseph Robson a near illiterate mason from Carsethorn nearby, John Hill the head of an established joinery business at Juniper Green, Edinburgh, and Francis Kedslie, a trusted and experienced subordinate whose services as Clerk of Works had been secured by Bryce. With these men the story of Shambellie moves from its theoretical stage into the hard and at times frustrating world of Victorian builders, the confusion of delays, the rigours of bad weather and all the mess of actual construction.

The Contractors

TOWARDS the end of February 1856 William Stewart made a special trip to Edinburgh to see his architect. In September the previous year he had at last decided to go ahead and contractors had been approached. His purpose now was to go through the estimates for building the house and in the George Street office Stewart and Bryce sat down to do their sums. The memorandum which Bryce prepared afterwards gives the distinct impression that he had made every effort to lay the total possible expense before his client. The cost had floated up to £2,580, though by now it was a cost based, for the most part, on actual tenders submitted by tradesmen. As both men had been busy in getting estimates Stewart must have been pleased to find that it was his candidates, two local men, who were the cheapest. The contractors favoured by Bryce, Robert Hume and James McCandlish, had submitted tenders of £3,350 and £2,515.1.0 respectively while a collaboration between the Carsethorn mason Joseph Robson and the Dumfriesshire joiner John Mein worked out at a cost of £2,206. To this Bryce added the extras that his client might have overlooked: £27 for the bell-hanger; £25 for marble chimney pieces; £10 for encaustic tiles in the entrance hall; £150 for his own fees, inspection and travelling; £100 for the approach road which would have to be laid to the new site; and £50 to provide a water supply for the house.

To judge from subsequent events and correspondence there was a good deal of discussion at this meeting about possible further costs which still worried Mr Stewart, while Bryce queried the reliability of the local men who were unknown to him. Stewart assured Bryce that they were sound and gave him a note of the tenders which he had negotiated. On this basis the contracts began to be let but despite his client's assurances, Bryce soon ran into snags. Joseph Robson while 'very anxious to close the bargain' didn't seem to have done a job of this size before. He had no idea of the normal procedures and delayed several weeks before returning a formal acceptance of Bryce's offer of the masonry contract at £975.0.0. John Mein, with whom Stewart thought he had an informal arrangement, then refused the carpenter's contract unless he was given an extra allowance for felt deadening between the floors which had been specified by Bryce and which he had either not noticed or had ignored. To Stewart the joiner's hesitation could only be countered with a direct attack. He would hold him, he wrote in April 1856 'liable for all damages, loss or inconvenience' occasioned by what he could only describe as 'his *very*

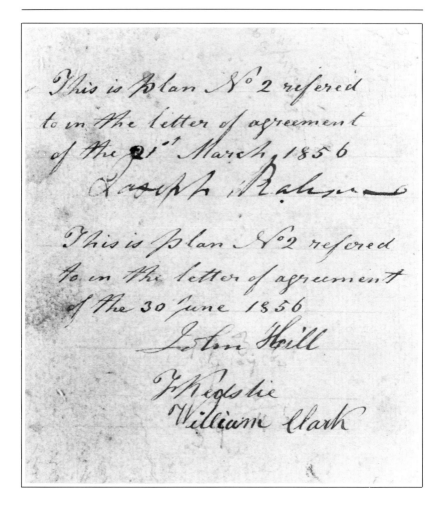

This is plan No 2 refered
to in the letter of agreement
of the 21st March 1856
Joseph Robson
This is plan No 2 refered
to in the letter of agreement
of the 30 June 1856
John Hill
F. Kedslie
William Clark

15. Detail of the endorsement of one of the working drawings for Shambellie. It will be noted that Joseph Robson the mason signed the plans in March 1856 whereas the other principal contractor, John Hill, and the Clerk of Works, Francis Kedslie were not appointed until June the same year. The identity of William Clark is not known.

dishonourable conduct', which piece of plain, disgruntled speech made Mein decline the contract absolutely. 'I am at a loss to understand upon what grounds you take the liberty of calling me dishonourable', he replied 'seeing that even now my estimate is not accepted either by yourself or Mr Bryce who acts for you. Mr Bryce has proposed to me terms of an agreement that I am at perfect liberty either to accept or decline and, for a variety of reasons, I do positively decline to accept the offer made to me by Mr Bryce'. And in refusing the carpentry contract he renounced the plastering and slating jobs as well.

Poor Mr Stewart was now in a most unenviable position. He had lost face with his architect in recommending, and that quite warmly, a man who proved unreliable and his thoughtless attempt to force the issue had only made matters worse. Moreover Mein had not asked for a very substantial allowance against the felt but one to which Bryce might well have been inclined to agree. We are left with the feeling that it was as much Mr Stewart's fussy confusion about the quality and value of the timber in his own woods, for he had re-embarked on this unpromising topic, now with the carpentry contractor, that precipitated Mein's change of heart. At any event the Dumfries joiner decided he did not want to work for the laird of Shambellie and there the matter rested.

But it could not rest long. The new mansion was already rising from its foundations, and Robson had to be supplied with moulds for the free-stone work which, according to his contract, the joiner at Shambellie was supposed to supply. Blunt and rough spoken, he now began to tax his employer with the inconveniences he suffered through the lack of a joiner on the site. He pestered Stewart, who in turn pestered Bryce, attempting in his embarassment to shift the blame to his architect for the contractual confusion he himself had caused. 'I am disappointed' he wrote on 14 May 1856, 'that you have not written me to say that the joiner and other contracts for the house are completed as Robson is very impatient to get the moulds.... I told him to write to you as you were wholly responsible for the contract and that it was *not* with my approbation you had sanctioned his proceeding with the mason work before all the other work was properly contracted for and the estimates agreed on—I shall be sorry to find you have any deficiency to make up but the thing is very awkward for all parties concerned'. No doubt Bryce would let him know in a day or two what he proposed to do.

The reply came by return. Bryce had found a joiner but the lowest tender he could get was £190.0.0 above Mein's estimate and unless some modification were made upon the plans it could not be less. He had also got a slater to roof the house at Mein's charge and Robson had agreed to take on the plasterwork. But the only way to reduce the joiner's charge would be to cut out the attic floor at present. As for Stewart's notions about his architect making up the difference in the price, these had to be scotched at once. Bryce had been riled by the very suggestion and now committed to paper, with forthright candour, his views on the whole job: 'I think it quite necessary to answer the latter part of your letter, to put an end to any misunderstanding. I have taken trouble about this building to meet your wishes, greatly beyond what I am ever called on to do, and if you expect that I am to make up any deficiency in the expense of the house, beyond what you intend to lay out you quite misunderstand my position. You put into my hands a parcel of estimates and repeatedly told me that Mein was willing and most anxious to go on with the work at a certain rate, and in faith of this I contracted with the mason also at the sum which has been agreed upon. But when Mein is called upon to fulfil his engagement, he declines unless an allowance is made to him; is it for a moment to be supposed that this allowance is to be made out of my pocket? The idea is absurd and I never, in the whole course of my experience heard of such a proposition; I therefore beg it distinctly to be understood that I will not be responsible in any way, for the work being completed, either at the estimated sums, or for the difference between Mein's estimate and any other that may be adopted'.

Was this letter sufficient to Bryce's needs or was he irritable and still out of sorts after it had been written? Did he vent his displeasure on some unfortunate draughtsman in the outer office or quietly confide in J. C. Walker, his senior clerk, who had a good deal to do with the Shambellie business. A quick reply is usually an indication that Bryce felt threatened, for when things went well the office correspondence was conducted at a comfortable, almost easy going pace. It was a norm with Bryce to promise replies within a week yet to let fifteen or twenty days slip by before he took any action. In 1861 the secretary of the New Club in Edinburgh had a minor problem with the cisterns that fed the members' baths and, though the club in Princes Street was just round the corner from the office, he had had to wait several months before the architect's attention could be brought to focus on the members' needs. Bryce at bay is a different character; he becomes emphatic and prompt.

Now letters pass rapidly between the two men. The very next day, Stewart writes that he is astonished 'after all that has passed' and his 'repeated warnings not to run into more expense' that Bryce, who had no authority from him should have behaved in such an unbusiness-like way. Didn't he understand that, having started with one contractor before the others had signed, Stewart, as client, was now completely at the tradesmen's mercy? Surely Bryce would agree to reduce his fees to £100—'in equity' that was due to Stewart—or should they not prosecute Mein if it were really his fault? Bryce in reply denied that he had led Stewart into further expense. The muddle with Mein was of his client's making and he certainly would not reduce his fees. There was nothing now that Stewart could do but give up the attics and accept whatever reduction in the joiner-work Bryce might suggest. 'It is useless to extend this correspondence', he ended on 23 May 1856, 'for the time is now come when the work must proceed'. Robson was asking every day for a joiner on the site and Bryce had done nothing about it!

Bryce was at this time off on a visit to more congenial jobs so it fell to James Campbell Walker to answer Stewart's missive. He wrote at once to say that John Hill, the Edinburgh contractor who had agreed to take on the joinery, was out of town but that the reduced specification was with the quantity surveyor, William Lawrence, that it should come within his cost, and that it would be sent as soon as possible. But when Bryce returned, the tone of his client's last letter seemed to demand a very particular reply. Things were not as they seemed. He had been busy on his client's behalf. He had found contractors for the outstanding departments of the building work and he had had enough: 'The disagreeable correspondence, which has commenced for the second time, and the unfounded allegations you make are such that, with any pleasure or comfort to myself, I cannot continue longer to conduct the works at Shambellie. I beg therefore to withdraw my services, and hope in the course of tomorrow to be able to send you Mr Lawrence's report on the reduction of the estimate for the carpenter and joiner works'. Two days later Lawrence's report was sent along with the names and addresses of all the contractors—'first rate men' with whom Stewart should have no difficulty in dealing. The final drawings would follow the next week and Bryce was thankful to be now 'relieved of this business'.

The House goes up

THE building works at Shambellie had been in hand for no more than six weeks before Mr Stewart's peevish complaints provoked the resignation of his architect. Bryce had visited the site on a Friday in the middle of April 1856. Typically he was in a rush. He arrived in Dumfries off the Lockerbie Coach just before one o'clock and was at once driven to Shambellie where, with

Joseph Robson in attendance, he set out the foundations the same afternoon and immediately returned to Dumfries so as to be able to catch the first train in the morning to go to Capenoch, near Thornhill (where he was adding a new baronial tower to the house) and still get back by public transport to Edinburgh the same night. Mr Stewart may well have felt the visit was a bit too quick but that was Bryce's way.

   Mein had attended at the site meeting, but immediately after the problem of additions to his contract had arisen, and he resigned the job. Now at the end of May it was Bryce who left his client, or intended to leave, for one of the most inexplicable aspects of the Shambellie story is that Bryce's resignation was not effective. Mr Stewart ignored it. The architect's letter is preserved amongst the building papers for the house but there is no evidence that Stewart ever acknowledged it. On the contrary he merely wrote a week later on 7 June to say that the joiner had arrived from Edinburgh and that he and Robson were making arrangements for scaffolding and for erecting the mason's sheds. As all the papers were later to be submitted to Stewart's lawyer in Edinburgh it is just possible that *amour propre* led him to extract the copy of his own apology with Bryce's retraction of his resignation. With so much else laid open in the correspondence it seems odd that he should do so, yet equally it is out of character for David Bryce to allow himself to be beaten, in a matter touching both his reputation and convenience. Perhaps Mr Stewart paid a second visit to the George Street office and settled the disagreement in person.*

   Whatever was agreed, the construction of Shambellie was soon proceeding rapidly. By the end of June Robson was due the second instalment for the masonry, payable when the walls had reached the bedroom floor level, and on 5 July Francis Kedslie, the Clerk of Works, made the first of what were to be nine visits to inspect the house. He spent two days at Shambellie, sending in a very favourable report of Robson's work at the end of his visit. Throughout the summer all went well: by the end of July the joists of the first floor were in place; Kedslie paid a second visit to inspect the work in the third week of August; and by late October Robson had the shell of the house virtually complete. The contractors were favoured by mild weather in the autumn which, continuing throughout November, allowed John Hill to have the roof finished and ready for the slates by the end of that month.

---

*Since this account was written William Stewart's diary for 1856 has come to light: the entry for 5th June is as follows 'To travel to and from Edinburgh and three days there seeing Mr Bryce and Mr Duncan regarding Mansion House for joiner work etc. £3.11s.4d.'

Traditional Scottish roof construction differs from what is normally found in England or Ireland, in that the rafters are covered not merely with narrow horizontal slips of timber but with a continuous surface of smooth boarding—like a sloping floor—on which the tiles or slates are laid. This boarding, known as 'sarking', makes for a very firm and warm structure. Bryce, in keeping with the building tradition in which he was brought up, specified such a roof for Shambellie and it was a roof of rafters and sarking which Hill completed in November 1856. In normal cirumstances the use of sarking can only improve a building yet, as was sadly so often the case with Mr Stewart's house, a good beginning was to end badly. The first hint of trouble is contained in a note from J. C. Walker to Stewart, dated 4 December, confirming that 'the lead and slates were shipped from Glasgow' a week before and that they should 'now be very near their destination'. But the lead and slates did not come. On Boxing Day Stewart wrote to Bryce to say that there had been two slaters at Shambellie for a fortnight but still 'no intelligence of the vessel', and it was not until a week later that Bryce heard a report that the ship had been obliged 'by stress of weather' to put back to Lamlash, on Arran Island, and had thus a good three-quarters of its journey still to complete. For more than a month the house stood finished except for the covering on its roof, while the bad weather, which had forced the brig back into the Firth of Clyde, struck the whole of the South West. Conducted by the sarking huge volumes of water now came pouring onto the tops of the walls, washing out the pointing and causing such settlement that a number of the sills and lintels of the windows cracked. For a further fortnight no news was heard of the cargo of slates and lead, while one of the masons at Shambellie told Mr Stewart, to his great alarm, that he thought 'the walls had suffered as much in the last two months exposure as if they had been built for 20 years and properly protected'. After some weeks of bad weather a man was sent up to the roof to strip the sarking back to before the wall head so that the main body of water could fall harmlessly through the building, but by then the walls had suffered considerable damage. The brig never reached New Abbey but putting out again later in January was wrecked in the Solway firth with the loss of its cargo and all hands. Before this sad news reached either Shambellie or Edinburgh, Bryce had compelled the contractor to send fresh slates to Dumfries by rail and the house was properly roofed by the beginning of March.

While these problems came and went, relations between Mr Stewart and his architect had suffered another setback: there had been a skirmish about fees. In September Bryce had sent in a bill for the two sets of designs he had

prepared accompanied by a note that it was 'usual to receive a payment to account for plans' when buildings were at the stage which Shambellie then was. Mr Stewart promptly paid the bill for the second set with an order on the British Linen Company for sixty pounds, but ignored the request for payment for the first set. Bryce sent a receipt by return and again asked for payment for the first design. His letter was ignored. In October, fearing that the post had miscarried, he wrote again and this time drew upon himself expressions of exasperation and dismay so clearly tinged with criticism that the letter can only have irritated its recipient: 'I hope you will reconsider your claim for *two sets* of Plans, which I think most unfair, as the first were rejected through no fault of mine but as unsuitable in point of extent and expense for the kind of house for which I instructed you to prepare plans: and had I not been under the impression that you were not to charge me for the first, if I employed you for a new set of plans for a smaller scale of house, I certainly should never have gone further with you'. Mr Stewart was surprised that Bryce should be 'so pressing for any more money in the meantime' and in support of his view of the case made reference to his brother-in-law, 'present in the room at the time I returned the first set of plans', who had the same impression as himself.

Now Bryce was entirely within his rights. When asked to prepare a second design, he had written in the spring of 1855 to say he would do so but that the first set would have to be paid for. The design had been carried to the stage of full working drawings and a specification, and Mr Stewart, if he had cared to look it up, had the letter amongst the other correspondence about the house. Bryce now stood firm: 'Both you and your brother are labouring under a mistake in supposing that I said I would give the first plans gratuitously', he wrote on 6 October 1856: 'I distinctly remember what I said, which was, that I never had a quarrel with my employers about fees and that I would make my charges as easy as possible'. He was quite prepared to wait for payment if that might be more convenient for his client but he would not let the matter stand over to be challenged later. In the face of this rock-like intransigence Mr Stewart capitulated though, as there is no pleasure in business relationships of this sort, the matter left more than a little resentment on his side.

Because of the delay of the slates Shambellie was now badly behind schedule and in a poor state. When Bryce issued a certificate for the slater, William Anderson of Edinburgh, Mr Stewart refused to pay it until he had been satisfied who was to be held responsible for the delay and loss. Robson should have been finished by 1 April and Hill by 1 May, yet both were behind as were

16. Shambellie, Winter 1856–57.

the plasterers and plumbers and each blamed the other for delays. In truth the whole contract was in a mess. The unfortunate events of the winter had given every tradesman a perfect excuse for ignoring the deadlines of the contracts, and Stewart was entirely dependent on Bryce to see that things moved ahead at all. In the middle of May he wrote to ask if he could come down: he was not pleased with the slates and the mason work was not looking very well. Bryce sent Kedslie instead and towards the end of July Stewart wrote again. He wanted to get on with the grounds and terraces but Robson hadn't filled in the foundations and the keying and pointing of the masonry had still to be done. There were 'one or two things' with which he was not satisfied and 'a seasonal visit from the architect' might, he thought, 'be beneficial'. Even after this request Bryce did not go down to the South West and it was not until mid autumn, on 16 October, that he finally made a visit to the house.

To judge from the certificates and receipts that have survived, Shambellie was by then virtually finished. Bryce had issued certificates on the completion of work for the slater in April and for the plumber and plasterer—John McIllwrath of Ayr and James Anderson—on 6 July. Robson had had all but his last installment for the mason work and the carpentry and joinery contractor, John Hill, received his penultimate certificate for £200, which was due 'when all the floors are laid, the windows glazed and hung, the doors hinged and the finishing in hand', on 7 December 1857. While Bryce was at Shambellie, the outside doors and windows were being painted for a mere £3.3.8. and Mr Stewart had already contracted with a monumental mason in Carlisle, James Carruthers, for three marble chimney pieces for the main rooms of the house. The operations had, it is true, extended to over twenty months, whereas Bryce had expected the main contractors to be finished within a year, yet as 1858 approached William and Katherine Stewart could be fairly sure that the next six or eight months would see them safely installed in their new home.

Disagreements

VERY little has been preserved among the Shambellie papers for 1858. Mr Carruthers came with his chimney pieces from Carlisle and, after a slight misunderstanding about the cost of the design for the drawing-room, was paid the full sum of £30.0.8. on 9 September. The encaustic tiles in the hall were laid by a Mr G. H. Potts from Edinburgh in June and the bells were hung by the appropriately named Robert Bell from Dumfries for £25.0.0. Mr Stewart had toyed with the idea of installing gas lighting but gave it up as too expensive. By October the whole house had been papered and painted at a cost of £48.12.6. There are fragmentary hints, in letters from Bryce's office, that Robson's work had not been satisfactory, that the walls leaked in places and that he had been dilatory in finishing outstanding jobs about the building, but there is nothing to indicate the true position at Shambellie until a letter from Katherine Stewart on 22 January 1859 brings the family's situation vividly to life:

> 'Mr Stewart is so much annoyed and disgusted with the state of the house that I cannot prevail upon him again to write you on the subject. Now out of consideration not only for the furniture but for the health of the family I am reduced to trouble you and to beg that something may immediately be done to prevent the rain completely destroying the house. We have not a habitable room to sit in and all the bedrooms (particularly the one we occupy) has literally been all the week in one continued pour. The ceilings and walls are suffering very much and it appears to me that not only the mason work but the slates and plumbers work as well are defective. Qualified workmen under the inspection of the clerk of works or some fully qualified person should immediately be sent to put things to rights—Robson sent two men about a fortnight ago to do what was necessary but after cementing one or two crevices they left and it has been *worse* than it was before they were here. Should something not be immediately done we shall certainly have to leave the house as we are all suffering more or less from the continued damp. An answer by return of post saying what is to be done will oblige'.

William Stewart was unusually fussy, too fastidious to find satisfaction in the practical pursuit of an architectural ideal and too petulant—perhaps too formal—to put workmen at their ease or to enjoy their confidence. He seems to have lacked personal authority; certainly he let grievances weigh in his mind too long. A more positive personality might have come through the Shambellie business better, yet, in the design and building of his family home, he had been visited with disappointments and humiliations that might have broken a stronger man. The house he had built cost much more than he intended; it had taken too long to build; it had led him into acrimonious disputes in which he had come off badly and, now that it was built, it proved neither wind nor water tight. The chimneys did not draw, the boiler did not heat the water properly, and no one, tradesmen, clerk of works or architect, could be brought to acknowledge a share in the blame or to act to remedy these faults.

Robson, the mason, was the greatest problem. Even Bryce admitted that he was 'at a loss what to do with him' as he paid no attention to repeated letters and could not be brought to repair faults in the walls or finish minor jobs. But Bryce himself continued to treat his clients in a cavalier way. In reply to Mrs Stewart's letter he wrote that Francis Kedslie was too busy on another job in Caithness to make a special visit to Shambellie but that he would 'send a person to see what is wrong and he would stay and see it put right'. Later in April Mr Stewart wrote to ask why Bryce had done nothing about the house and again in July to remind him that he had promised, when the Stewarts had made a visit to the office in Edinburgh, that he would send the clerk of works along with several contractors by the middle of June to see the work properly done'. Robson had finally agreed to come and do a little work in May but the house was still leaking very generally.

It was not until 27 July 1859 that Kedslie at last wrote to Stewart to make arrangements for his visit: he could only be away from his current job at Stirkoke House near Wick for a brief period, and Mr Stewart would have to get two casks of Portland cement—Baryley White Brothers or G & T Earle Hulls would be best—before he came. He would require 'active masons with ladders and scaffolding ready to begin operations' as soon as he arrived and 'two or three carts of pure fresh-water sand'. There was no use in his coming until everything was on the spot. Mr Stewart would have to order it himself or authorise Kedslie to get it. The tone of the note, busy and perhaps just a little disrespectful, provoked the predictable reaction from poor Mr Stewart who by now seemed incapable of seeing where his own interest lay: 'I have yours of the 27th ult and would have you communicate with Mr Bryce with whom rests the entire direction and responsibility of having the contracts completed and giving me a good and habitable house. It cannot be supposed that I am to pay for insufficiently executed work and I have suffered enough already, which might all have been avoided by proper attention at first'. So Kedslie postponed his visit. It would have cost William Stewart little trouble and less money to lay in the materials and get the work done, yet such was his nature, or his sense of grievance, that he would stand upon his dignity rather than move even to serve his own ends, while the practical men with whom he had to deal can only have wondered at his querulousness. In the event it was not until early October that Kedslie was able to visit Shambellie to report on the cause of Stewart's complaints, a full eight months after Katherine Stewart's appeal to Bryce for help. By then Mr and Mrs Stewart had been exposed to nuisance and annoyance in their house for so long that it was inevitable they should expect the clerk of works to endorse their complete dissatisfaction yet Kedslie's report of 18 October 1859 was surprisingly mild.

What Robson had done in May was to rake out all the joints in the masonry and to repoint the south and west fronts, which were the most exposed, with Portland cement and the east and north with lime mortar. In October Kedslie had shown him some places that should be done again but he had absolutely refused to do any more at the house and another mason, James Lewis, had been called in to rectify parts of the pointing. Some lintels and window sills were cracked. For the most part Mr Stewart would take a reduction for them rather than insist on their replacement and they could be cemented up. Kedslie found the roof in perfect order. As Anderson had a slater at the house he had, as a precaution, asked him to re-bed all the ridge stones and gable skews in cement instead of lime. As for Mr Stewart's complaint that his bath would not fill and that the boiler failed to heat the water these were minor matters and could easily be remedied. The servants had not realised that there was a stop cock to vent the hot water system and an air lock had prevented the water getting to the bath, while 'the want of fuel on the fire' was the most obvious reason for the low temperature of the water! The joiner work, which was also a cause of complaint, amounted to no more than a few 'trifles' resulting from some of the door latches being muddled when they had been removed by the painter who decorated the rooms. John Hill could correct this at once.

When Bryce forwarded Kedslie's report to his clients he found the Stewarts in no mood to accept a series of such simple arguments in explanation of their complaints. Things were very much worse than they sounded here. It was now December and renewed wet weather had again reduced them to 'a miserable state of discomfort'. Bryce referred their reply to Kedslie who stood firm taking all protestations of discomfort with a grain of salt. When he was at the house in October, he had asked particularly about Robson's re-pointing and neither Mr or Mrs Stewart had been able to show him any leak or damp in the wall 'with the exception of Mrs Stewart thinking she heard a drop' and that, he added, could not be traced: 'Mr Stewart states the walls, slates, sashes are all at fault. I am very sorry that one drop of water should make its appearance but have no hesitation in saying there is a good sprinkling of exaggeration in these statements'.

By the autumn of 1859 William Stewart was ready to embark on another line of attack. If Bryce and Kedslie could not be relied upon for proper support he would take other advice. There was in Dumfries a very reliable Civil Engineer called Andrew Scott. Mr Stewart invited him to Shambellie, showed him the faults of which he complained and, we may imagine, poured into his attentive ear the long history of abuses and ill usage to which he was subjected during the conduct of the works. Mr Scott, accompanied by experienced tradesmen, inspected Shambellie late in November, on Boxing Day 1859 and again on 6 January 1860. He counted sixteen broken sills and lintels and noted 'many of the rebates, piers, mullions and string mouldings much fractured caused evidently from bad setting and unequal safeing of the free-stone work'. In the re-pointing Robson had not properly cleaned out the joints; there was 'very general leakage all over the roof' and the slates were the wrong sort and colour to those specified in the contract. Nor had the nails used on the roof been properly steeped in oil. Now this was exactly the sort of report that Mr Stewart wanted. A certain note of triumph creeps into his next communication with Bryce written on 9 January 1860: 'the cause of the wet getting into my house will be best understood by you by seeing the enclosed Report of an Architect to whom I submitted the specifications and copies of the several reports by Kedslie and who has carefully examined the house and seen the state it was in. It would appear very reprehensible of Mr Kedslie allowing such work to pass unnoticed and I feel that I have been very much trifled with in the delay that had taken place between tradesmen and clerk of works etc., who only seem to cloak one another. Now that you know the true state of matters I shall expect you to give me immediate redress'.

Bryce had not been at Shambellie for well over two years. Inevitably he passed Mr Stewart's letter together with Scott's report to Kedslie who was not well pleased to see his own competence impugned. As the house had stood with the sarking exposed in the winter of 1857, Scott took the view that the slating contractor was partly to blame for the damage to the walls—an opinion that Stewart also held—but Kedslie would have none of it. He had already settled the matter before and asked now why Scott 'when he was listening to Stewart's dictation' did not ask himself where the leakage first appeared and whether it was the lack of slates which 'brought all the pointing off the gables and chimney stalks' whose exposed faces were just as bad as the wall head. As for the slates Mr Stewart knew very well that Bryce had allowed the contractor to substitute Roseneath in place of the slates specified which had been lost in the wreck and could not be replaced. Kedslie was sure the workmanship was sound; if there were leaks it was because the gutters had been allowed to be choked with leaves and snow and had never been cleaned out, besides there had been all sorts of other workmen tramping over the roofs since they were finished in 1858. 'It cannot be imagined for one moment', he added, 'that in a job that lasted for about two years, where I have only paid eight visits, that I could see everything right, especially with tradesmen such as you had at Shambellie'.

While Kedslie was composing this reply in Caithness, Bryce had had two callers in his office in Edinburgh. The first was Joseph Robson who had come to seek a certificate for payment of the final installment of his contract and who had been told by Bryce that he would have to replace the two worst lintels at Shambellie at a time when Bryce would send down a Clerk, James Kay, to superintend the work. The second visitor was James Duncan of 6 Hill Street, Edinburgh, a senior partner in Duncan & Dewar and the Shambellie family's lawyer. He had received a letter from William Stewart complaining about Bryce, who would not send back some plans, about the mason and the slater, from all of which it was evident that Stewart was spoiling for a row. Old Mr Duncan, in a long practice, had acquired some wisdom in human affairs and his letter to his disgruntled client is worth quoting in full:

> 'I am favoured with your letter this morning, and regret to learn that there are any misapprehensions between you and the builder, as well as the slater. But I shall confine myself to the plans, and the agreement about the slater work. You are aware that I have long been acquainted with Mr Bryce, so that instead of writing him it seemed to me to be better to go round to George Street, whence I have just returned.
>
> As to the plans, he states, after conversing with his Clerk, that Nos 5 & 12 are in your own possession, or at least, that they have never been returned. The others he is to send you. But Mr Kedslie, who is in the North, has had the Dumfries report communicated to him, and the plans would have been sent immediately, only Mr Bryce would prefer to retain them until he hears from Mr Kedslie.
>
> As to the slater work, when handing me the accompanying copy of the offer of 3 May 1856, Mr Bryce explained, in very distinct terms, that subsequent to that date, it had been arranged that Roseneath slates should be substituted for those estimated—that the vessel freighted with Roseneath slates had gone down to the great loss of the contractor, who did his best to get the loss repaired, and who is said to be a first rate tradesman, and who for a long period of years has conducted himself to the entire satisfaction of Mr

Bryce. He seemed to feel very much for Mr Anderson who has been a great loser by the job.

It is due to Mr Bryce to say that he received me very politely and very cordially. Though annoying to be troubled with such things as necessarily arise in the building of a mansion house, I suspect that the only way to deal with them is to make sacrifices as the effectual way of getting rid of them. Permit me to say that it is not for your interest to get into discussions with the slater, for there is a distinction between such a fatality as a vessel being wrecked, and a tradesman delaying to perform his work from carelessness and indifference. The inconvenience may be as great in the one case as in the other but both a judge and a jury would recognise the distinction.

I get on pretty well with Mr Bryce, and it occurs to me that he may feel a little at your passing him over because it is desirable that he should dispose of such differences. You know my maxim, which I rather think I have quoted to you, and almost daily act upon, that enlightened liberality, in good time, is real economy in the end. Pardon my writing you this freely, and believe me, with kindest regards to Mrs Stewart, and though somewhat late all the best wishes of the season to her and yourself, as well as all the members of your interesting family — James Duncan'.

Within two days of the writing of this letter events at Shambellie took such a disastrous turn as to carry William Stewart well beyond the reach of Mr Duncan's moderate views and practical good advice. On the morning of Tuesday, 16 January Robson had appeared at the house, with workmen ready to replace the two cracked lintels under the inspection of a clerk of works. He had not bothered to tell Bryce that he was coming and, as a result, there was no one there to oversee the work. William and Katherine Stewart had to cope as best they could on their own, and Mr Stewart became so upset at what happened that once more it was Katherine who had to communicate the course of events to Bryce. Robson's men began by dressing the lintels on the lawns of the terrace outside the house. When Mr Stewart objected because it was destroying the grounds and asked them to lay boards below the stones, they would not do so nor would they stop and Robson meanwhile began to demolish the wall. Stewart then told him that he considered that he was wrong to proceed without the clerk of works, the more so as Mr Kedslie had said it would not be safe to remove the lintels even in the autumn. When Robson persisted Stewart had warned him 'that what he was doing was entirely at his own risk, and on his own responsibility', upon which Robson lost his temper, 'became very impertinent, threw down his tools and said he would do no more'. He had smashed the old lintels on the pretence of repairing them but could not be got even to make up the wall again, and the ground-floor laundry window was left standing open and 'in a very exposed state'. If something were not to be done at once 'Mr Stewart must apply to the Sheriff'.

Settling the Accounts

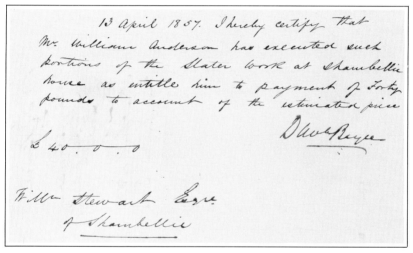

17. A certificate issued by David Bryce on 13 April 1857 for part of the slater work by William Anderson at Shambellie. William Stewart refused to pay.

13 April 1857. I hereby certify that Mr William Anderson has executed such portions of the slater work at Shambellie House as entitle him to payment of Forty pounds to account of the estimated price
£40.0   David Bryce
Willm Stewart Esqre
of Shambellie

JOSEPH Robson's alarming display of temper at Shambellie confirmed Mr. Stewart in a course of action that he had been contemplating since the beginning of 1860. He would withdraw entirely from the final stages of completing his house and of settling the accounts with the contractors. To this end he approached his lawyer in Dumfries, Robert K. Walker, who lived in the western suburb of Maxwelltown, asking him to act on his behalf. 'It will be very hard if there is no redress to be had either against the architect or

18. The Shambellie Stair Hall from a photograph taken in about 1890.

the contractors', he wrote in a letter enclosing copies of his most recent correspondence about the house. 'Bryce has been most indifferent and careless throughout and there is no getting him to insist on the house being completed or to attend to letters as you will see'. As for Robson, there was no telling what he'd do next and 'he should not be allowed to run riot without a check'. Indeed William Stewart now refused to meet the mason on any pretext. When, later that year, Robson came to Shambellie to let him know that to get matters settled he was willing to put in the lintels, word was sent out from the house that Mr Stewart would not see him and that he should address himself to his lawyer.

Thus the direction of the Shambellie contracts passed into other hands, and Robert Walker, at least to some extent, shouldered the responsibilities that Bryce had apparently evaded. The involvement of a third party, new alike to the job and to the disputes that centered on it, protracted rather than

19. David Bryce's fees from the pocket book in which William Stewart kept track of the cost of Shambellie.

		D Bryce Esqre Architect's account	£	S	D
1856 Septr. 17		To account of Plans etc	60	0	0
1863		To Order for same	0	1	7
April 16		To balance of account including £50 for first set of Plans & which were rejected	126	5	4
		To Postage of letter with cheque for the amount to Messrs Duncan & Dewar	0	0	4
			186	7	3

accelerated the resolution of Mr Stewart's problems: very soon the lawyer himself was to receive just those urgent notes, now hectoring, now peevish, which, in the past, had done so much to alienate architect and tradesmen, yet somehow he found the patience to placate his client and with it the means to bring matters to an end. He dealt with Bryce, with his new clerk John Paris and with the clerk of works who had replaced Kedslie, James Kay. Kay believed that the water came in through the walls—not the roof which was perfect—and Bryce advised that Robson, or failing him another mason, should be required to re-point the house again. This was also the opinion of William Reid Corson, an architect at 20 Cooper Street, Manchester, to whom Walker turned for advice. Corson's report on the house, while not quite exonerating Bryce, very much supports his view that poor mason work was the main fault; if his letter was shown to Mr Stewart, it must certainly have given him cause for reflection. Shambellie is built of two stones—granite on the walls and red Dumfriesshire sandstone on the worked sections such as the door and window surrounds. Bryce had strongly advised against adopting such a mixture, but as the sandstone was easier to work and therefore cheaper Stewart had ignored his architect's advice. Now W. R. Corson endorsed Bryce's view: 'It would be very difficult to saddle the slater with the responsibility of having spoiled the mason work by his delay', he wrote on 16 May 1860. 'My impression is that very much of the mischief arises from the difficulty, always existing in a building partly granite and partly freestone, of keeping the rain out where these meet, as in lintels and sills. Necessarily a cavity has to be left between them until the walls have settled, and then, when pointed there is a difficulty in making a water-tight joint between the two surfaces greater than exists where freestone alone has been used. Probably year by year the leakage will be less but the annoyance in the meantime is great'. In his view the only solution was to re-point again and as Bryce had reported that Robson's work after Kedslie had left 'was a mere sham' there was some hope that a better mason might do a better job. R. K. Walker contracted with a local builder in Dumfries, James Montgomery, to re-point the whole house with mastic and to replace the two smashed lintels and the sill of the dining-room window. Andrew Scott, the local engineer whose earlier report had so annoyed Francis Kedslie, agreed to supervise this work, and though Mr Stewart fretted dreadfully about his lawyer's delays and their missing 'the first tract of dry weather', the job was done by 27 July 1860.

The time was long past when Bryce could have been expected to oversee work at the house himself yet he remained protective towards the unfortunate

20. George McCallum, Bust of David Bryce in 1868

William Anderson, the Edinburgh slater whom he had asked to take on the roofing contract, and who, though he had lost some £36 on the job, was still being pursued by an indignant William Stewart wanting 'proper redress'. Independent reports on the roof had found it to be both sound and executed in a workmanlike manner and Corson had advised Walker 'by all means to avoid going to law with the slater'. But William Stewart, goaded relentlessly by his sense of personal injury, insisted that at least all the slates whose colour did not match should be changed. Anderson agreed to this and carried out the work, at his own expense, in August the same year. On balance he seems to have been unfairly, or at least ungenerously, treated. He had taken on a contract at a modest rate, possibly even to accommodate Bryce, and he had been a loser by it. It is true that the slates which he was asked to remove had been more expensive than those by which they were replaced so he perhaps was able to recoup a portion of his loss by his willing compliance with Mr

Stewart's demands. Nevertheless the Shambellie business had dragged on over many years and was to continue longer before accounts were settled. We are left with the impression that, in the case of William Anderson, the tradesman conducted himself with greater dignity and came out of the affair with more honour than did the gentlemen with whom he had to deal.

By the autumn of 1860 everything had been set right at the house. The damp papers had been removed from the walls and the rooms were completely redecorated. All was now ready for the final settlement of the various contractors' bills except that William Stewart would not pay up. Perhaps he felt he should see another winter out before he resigned the only possible sanction there remained to ensure the proper completion of his house. Or did he give in to some general feelings of resentment which allowed him a little satisfaction in the knowledge that the tradesmen were waiting for their cash? Perhaps, most probably of all, he was inclined to dispute minor sums in each account. Anderson, Hill and McIlwrath all sent in bills with letters requesting payment while Robson, the villain of the piece, had the temerity to claim various extra charges, principally for working the walls in square faced rubble instead of rough rubble, though he absolutely refused to make any allowance for the substitution of sandstone instead of granite for the wrought portions of the work. It was Robson who finally brought matters to a head. There are amongst the building papers several letters by him, the most expressive of which is the brief message scrawled on a torn sheet 'James, Say to Mr Stewart if he is not willing to pay the account he may depend I will give it into a hand that will sone [sic] settle it'. While William Stewart contemplated a variety of actions his builder took him to court.

The summons, which was sent on 12 November 1861, found Mr Stewart in a defiant, almost exultant, mood: Robson's account was wildly wrong and Stewart was confident he 'should have no difficulty in more than counter-balancing the very extravagant and imaginary claims' he made and in forcing him or his guarantors 'to pay heavy damages for non fulfillment of the contract'. Yet there are always two versions of any dispute and Robson's lawyer, who had taken the precaution of obtaining written statements from the men who had worked on the walls, had 'not the slightest doubt of Mr Stewart's liability'. In the event it was the lawyer who was proved to be right. The case was heard on 19 March 1862 by Lord Kinloch who awarded a decree for certain sums for Robson. Stewart appealed to the first division of the Court of Session but before the case came up the moderate counsels of the family lawyers had at last prevailed and the parties agreed to settle by a joint minute that was merely reported to Lord President McNeil on 4 July 1862. In the interim between the case and the appeal Messrs. Duncan and Dewar had been instructed to settle the outstanding tradesmen's accounts paid between 21 June and 2 July that year. Bryce and Kedslie had however to wait until April 1863 before the balance of their bills of £147.5.4. and £19.5.6 was paid and with that their connection with Shambellie ends. About this time Mr Stewart did a little calculation of what the house had cost him which he computed to have been £2,984.10.9 exclusive of legal fees and the cost of the court case.

Epilogue

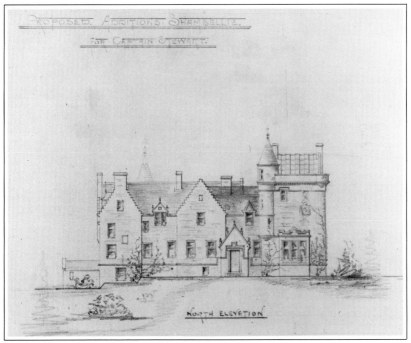

21. Elevation of a scheme to extend Shambellie in 1897.

Is it fanciful in recounting a story of this sort to imagine that Bryce's client learnt something of human nature during the construction of his house? The subsequent history of Shambellie seems to suggest that he did. Though he

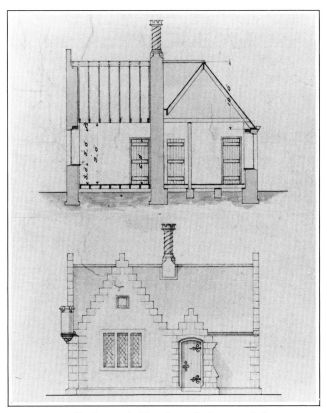

22. Section and Elevation of the gate lodge at Shambellie designed by John Barbour in 1863.

was never to see Bryce or Kedslie again (for family tradition has kept alive the memory of their great antipathy) Mr Stewart had more building work to carry out on his estate for the direction of which he now looked no further than Dumfries. The work was of course more modest than the mansion house had been but where that was attended with frustration and loss, this proceeded easily and accounts were settled at once. A stable yard had been built close to the road near New Abbey to a plan by Andrew Scott about 1859 and in April 1863 the gate and gate lodge were designed by John Barbour, an architect at 27 Buccleuch Street, Dumfries. The lodge, a pretty three-roomed cottage built in granite, with crow-stepped gables and twisted chimney pots, cost £210.8.4.

23. Children at Shambellie climbing the ivy on the house.

None of the men who built it had worked for Mr Stewart before. It went up quickly in the autumn of 1863 and was paid for entirely by 20 February 1864. Two years later Mr Barbour also advised on fitting up the attics, a job which cost a total of £76.3.0, on which he charged a fee of two guineas, and with this done Shambellie was at last complete. In 1897 William's eldest son, Captain William Stewart, toyed with the idea of enlarging the house by building a four-storey baronial tower to the right of the entrance porch immediately west from the library. Sketch plans showing the addition, which was to have provided a

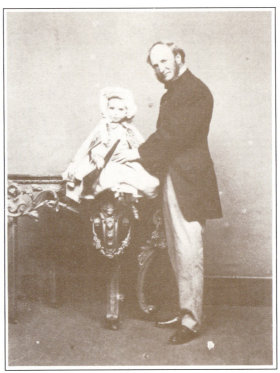

24. William Stewart with his youngest child, Nina, photographed about 1865.

billiard room and cloakroom with bedrooms above, were drawn up, probably in Mr Barbour's office, but the scheme never got beyond the drawing board and Shambellie remains as Stewart and Bryce conceived it.

The architect must have seen the house for the last time on 9 May 1862 when, in preparation for the court action between Robson and Stewart, he came to make a report on the state of the building. Among his commissions, which by the end of his life were to exceed 230, the Kirkcudbrightshire house was one of the most modest and yet it had proved to be one of the most difficult jobs. Perhaps in this last visit Bryce was touched by William Stewart's predicament for, after rendering his final account, totalling £207 5s. 4d., he deducted the sum of 20 guineas, so that his final visit, the report he wrote, Kay's expenses for the last inspection and all the discussions with legal agents were, in effect, given free of charge.

25. Katherine Stewart shortly after Mr Stewart's death in 1874.

Thus Bryce quits the scene, too successful and altogether too big to have fitted comfortably into the world of minor lairds and merchants that made up Mr Stewart's society. Among the architects of Victorian Scotland he had had most panache and had consistently enjoyed the confidence of the nobility conducting, not only a series of commissions for big country houses but also, works of prodigal scale for the Dukes of Atholl and Hamilton, for the Marquess of Breadalbane, and for the Earls of Airlie, Dalhousie, Seafield and South Eske. And in his last years, with extraordinary late fecundity, it was Bryce who gave to Edinburgh its most enduring High Victorian Monuments: St. George's West Church, The Royal Infirmary, the piece of Roman Baroque theatre which is the Bank of Scotland on the Mound and the haunting silhouette of Fettes College brooding above the trees at Comely Bank. Of Bryce's architecture there is much to say yet of Bryce the man we would know very little save for his connection with William Stewart. Thus, almost by accident, a minor commission provides the only guide to the character of one of Scotland's most accomplished Victorian designers.

And what of the Stewarts at Shambellie? The development of family life in this mid-Victorian house carries our story beyond the history of architecture and building into a world of imagination and memories. Katherine and William Stewart were not quite in their forties when Shambellie began to be planned: William was over 51 before the attics were fitted up. It would no doubt be wrong to imagine that the irritations of building the house robbed him of any pleasure in it once complete or that the family which grew up there was an unhappy one. Some evidence of the Stewart's later life has come down to us in photographs: of William in frockcoat and grey trousers pictured with his little daughter Nina precariously balanced on an ornate table; of Katherine, after his death in 1874, dressed in widow's black; or later, of his grandchildren hanging like fairy lights on a tree as they climb the ivy on the walls of the house. Images such as these, with views taken in the furnished rooms of the draped piano, slatted venetian blinds, a vase of lupins, stuffed birds and curling stones in the hall, remind us that a country house is as much a family's home as a piece of period architecture, and that the story of a building is a matter of personalities as much as of projects and plans.

Shambellie, 1956.

A Note on Further Reading

IN 1976 to mark the centenary of the death of David Bryce the Department of Fine Art at the University of Edinburgh mounted an exhibition entitled *Mr. David Bryce*. The catalogue by Valerie Fiddes and Alistair Rowan gives full information on the architect with a descriptive list of all his known work. *The Dictionary of National Biography* entry on Bryce is by G. W. Burnett and draws largely on the obituary notices published in *The Scotsman* and *The Edinburgh Courant* of 8 May 1876 and in *The Builder* for 27 May the same year. There are articles on Bryce by Colin McWilliam, 'Monarchs of the Glen', *The Listener* 12 August 1954 and by Neil Jackson, 'David Bryce R.S.A', *Scottish Field*, September 1973. Capenoch and Castlemilk, two Scottish Baronial houses by Bryce are treated in *Country Life* 13 August 1970 and 11/18 August 1977. A notice of the Stewarts of Shambellie together with a family tree appears in 'The Stewarts of Shambellie', in *The Stewarts: An Historical & General Magazine for The Stewart Society* (Edinburgh), vol. 3, 24 August 1912, pp. 33–58.

Photographic Acknowledgements
1, 2, 7 A. C. Cooper.
6 Scottish National Portrait Gallery.
13 Royal Commission, Ancient & Historical Monuments of Scotland.
22 Antonia Reeve.
All the rest are by Ken Smith, Royal Scottish Museum.

Pen and ink drawings by Charles W. Stewart.

Permission to reproduce kindly granted by
The Scottish National Portrait Gallery (6 & 22).
Mr R. Gladstone (13).
Mr C. W. Stewart (1, 2, 7, 8, 16, 17, 18, 19, 23, 24, 25, heading, endpiece and back cover).

Crown copyright
Copyright for drawings: 16, heading and end-piece Charles W. Stewart.

ISBN No. 0 900733 24 1

Designed by The Royal Scottish Museum Design Department.
Printed in Scotland for H.M.S.O., by Buccleuch Printers D'd 8360160 1/82